Morris and Buddy

The Story of the First Seeing Eye Dog

Becky Hall

Illustrated by **Doris Ettlinger**

Albert Whitman & Company, Morton Grove, Illinois

For the guide dogs and their trainers.—B.H.

To Lise Gescheidt, who has loved all her German shepherds
from Flicka to Lena.—D.E.

Special thanks to Teresa Davenport and Bruce Johnson of The Seeing Eye, Morristown, New Jersey, and
to Bill Mooney, whose videotaped reenactments breathed life into the colorful stories about Morris Frank.
My son, Brooks, inspired the research when he shared a book with me about the first guide dogs.
Sherry Bicknell, a blind childhood acquaintance, played cards with my sister and me and in many ways
demonstrated her independence in a darkened world.
Thank you to Morris and Buddy for opening infinite possibilities for the visually impaired.
Finally, there is no finer editor than Abby Levine. Thank you for your attention to details
and for your dedication to excellence.

All events described in this book are true. A few conversations have been recreated in order to
convey the spirit of the characters and events. —B.H.

Library of Congress Cataloging-in-Publication Data

Hall, Becky, 1950-
Morris and Buddy: the story of the first Seeing Eye dog / written by Becky Hall; illustrated by Doris Ettlinger.
p. cm.
Includes bibliographical references.
ISBN-13: 978-0-8075-5284-1 (hardback)
1. Frank, Morris. 2. Guide dogs—Juvenile literature. 3. Blind—Biography—Juvenile literature. I. Ettlinger, Doris. II. Title.
HV1780.H35 2007 362.4'183—dc22 2006023398

Published in 2007 by Albert Whitman & Company, 6340 Oakton Street, Morton Grove, Illinois 60053-2723.
Published simultaneously in Canada by Fitzhenry & Whiteside, Markham, Ontario. All rights reserved. No part of this book
may be reproduced or transmitted in any form or by any means, electronic or mechanical, including photocopying, recording,
or by any information storage and retrieval system, without permission in writing from the publisher.
Printed in the United States.
10 9 8 7 6 5 4 3 2

The design is by Carol Gildar.

For more information about Albert Whitman & Company, please visit our web site at www.albertwhitman.com.

❧ Table of Contents ❧

1

Like a Package

*B*lind and alone, Morris Frank arrived in the port city of Le Havre, France, like a package. He was put in a shed full of baggage. Carts squeaked as they rolled past him. Shouting voices called out in French. He smelled the bodies of workers as they pushed him this way and that. As he waited to be taken to the Paris train, Morris felt helpless and stiff with fear.

It was 1928 and Morris Frank was twenty years old. It was four years since he had been hit in a boxing match—four years since his world went dark, four years since he lost his independence. But in that time, he had attended college at Vanderbilt University in Nashville, Tennessee, and he had sold insurance door to door, walking through neighborhoods and ringing strangers' doorbells.

His father hired people to take him wherever he needed to go.

It was hard to depend on others. One day a young attendant led Morris to the business district and then declared he wanted a raise. When Morris refused, the man disappeared, leaving him alone, lost and blind.

Morris was no stranger to blindness. His mother had become completely blind when he was three years old. He had been her guide for most of his youth. And he had lost the sight of his right eye at six, when he rode a horse into an overhanging tree limb.

From his mother he inherited a fighting spirit. When at sixteen Morris became totally blind from the boxing accident, he rejected helplessness. He refused to weave baskets or make brooms, acceptable jobs for the blind in those days. He insisted on leading a normal life. It was this energy and determination that would make Morris Frank the perfect champion for the blind.

2

A Surprising Invitation

Standing amidst the French hustle and bustle, Morris wondered, "How did I get myself into this?"

He remembered the November day he was returning from the train station in his hometown of Nashville, Tennessee. The man at the newsstand thrust into his hand a copy of a popular magazine called the *Saturday Evening Post.* He said, "Morris, there's an article here your father should read to you."

Morris was astonished when he heard what the author, Dorothy Harrison Eustis, had to say. The title of her article was "The Seeing Eye." Mrs. Eustis was a wealthy American dog trainer who lived near Vevey, Switzerland. She wrote about a school she had visited in Potsdam, Germany, where German shepherd dogs were

trained to help soldiers who had been blinded in World War I. The dogs guided the humans and became their eyes.

She described watching a man receive his guide dog. "One moment it was an uncertain shuffling blind man, tapping a cane, the next it was an assured person, with his dog firmly in hand and his head up, who walked toward us quickly and firmly, giving his orders in a confident voice."

Morris was stunned. He was excited and hopeful. Within days he had written a letter to Mrs. Eustis. He said, "I should like very much to forward this work in this country . . . at the age of sixteen I was deprived of my sight and know . . . what it means to be dependent on a paid helper."

Morris Frank made Dorothy Eustis think. She had been training her own dogs for police and army work. Her dogs found missing people, guarded buildings, and delivered messages. But when she read Morris's letter, she decided to help blind people, too. Dorothy Eustis invited Morris to Switzerland.

3

Welcome to Switzerland!

*T*hrilled about this possibility, Morris set off on his own. He was not allowed to travel independently as a sighted passenger would, so he was shipped by American Express from Nashville, just like a package. He traveled by steamship across the Atlantic Ocean.

On the ship an attendant led Morris into the dining room three times a day. For exercise he was walked on the decks of the ship. He was allowed to sit on a deck chair, but as soon as he got up, the attendant took him by the arm and led him back to his chair. In the evening, Morris was locked in his room for the night.

It was lonely, but he had time to imagine what his new life with a guide dog would be like. For hours he dreamed of traveling, working, speaking to groups—all on his own, without an attendant always by his side.

From Le Havre, Morris was taken to Paris where he was again locked in a room until the train's departure for Vevey, Switzerland. After several hours of traveling, he stepped off the train in Vevey. A gentle hand touched his arm. "Morris? Morris Frank?" a woman asked. "I am Dorothy Eustis and this is my head trainer and breeder, Jack Humphrey. Welcome to Switzerland, where we plan to change your life."

Morris thrust his hand out into the air. A small hand reached up and shook his. Morris noticed the firmness in Mrs. Eustis's grasp.

Jack Humphrey stepped forward to greet Morris. "You are the largest package we have ever received by American Express," he said, laughing.

Mrs. Eustis held Morris's elbow and led him to the car with confidence. She spoke to him without raising her voice, unlike so many people who treated a blind person as if he were also deaf. Jack Humphrey was jolly and talkative as they rode to Fortunate Fields, Mrs. Eustis's estate outside Vevey.

That day Dorothy Eustis and Jack Humphrey studied Morris. He was hunched over and hesitant in his movements. At dinner he fumbled with his food, but he

was good-natured and willing to take part in the meal-time joking. By coming to Switzerland, he had shown courage and a willingness to try new things. Dorothy Eustis and Jack liked Morris. He had passed his first test at Fortunate Fields.

Later Morris discovered that Elliott "Jack" Humphrey had helped Mrs. Eustis breed a pure line of German shepherds. Jack was strong-willed and hard-working. Although he did not have a formal education, he was a brilliant trainer who could teach animals to do seemingly impossible things. Once he had even trained a camel to walk backwards! After reading articles Jack had written about training German shepherds, Dorothy Eustis had invited him to Fortunate Fields.

Jack Humphrey and Dorothy Eustis were dedicated to breeding superior dogs that combined a good temperament, intelligence, strength, and endurance: perfect guide dogs for the blind.

4

Man Meets Dog

Morris moved into the Eustis estate, where he would stay for five weeks. The next day Jack said, "We have trained two dogs, Morris. After meeting you, we have chosen the one that will be a perfect match. Her name is Kiss."

Morris nearly choked.

"Kiss?" he asked. How embarrassing! How could a man have a dog named Kiss? He did not want to be ungrateful, but *Kiss?*

Morris thought, "I will be laughed out of Nashville if I call my dog Kiss. I can just imagine me saying, 'Kiss, here, Kiss, sit, Kiss, stay.'"

Jack ignored Morris's reaction and led the young man back to his bedroom. He said, "When I bring

Kiss to you, welcome her. Use her name. Play with her. Make her happy to be with you." He gave Morris a piece of meat for Kiss. Then Jack left to get the dog.

Morris waited, turning the meat over and over in his hands. He heard Jack's footsteps and the jangle of the dog leash. The door opened and Morris called, "Here, Girl." His voice was kind and gentle, but he did not call his new dog Kiss.

He opened his hand. He felt the dog's soft tongue and warm breath as she gently took the meat from his palm.

Morris ran his fingers over her head and down her back. Her cool nose was damp and her whiskers tickled his hand. Her ears were pointed and velvety. Her fur was soft. He felt the curve of her tail as it dipped down and back up. He put his arms around his dog and felt her tail wag slowly.

Morris Frank told his new companion, "Kiss is no name for *my* dog. From here on, you're Buddy."

5
The Work Begins

Dog and man had met. Now it was time to begin their education.

First Jack showed Morris the dog harness and leash. The stiff harness was just like the ones used with the guide dogs in Germany. It was designed so that the blind person could feel the dog's movements.

Morris had to practice putting on and taking off the harness. Several times he did it wrong and poked Buddy in the eye. He pinched her ear with the leather strap. He stepped on her paw. Throughout that first lesson, Buddy stood quiet and calm, allowing Morris to learn.

When the session was over, Morris said, "Okay, Jack. Now I'm ready. Let's go."

"No," said Jack. "A guide dog works for the approval

of the owner. She must get to know and love you first. At this point, Kiss—ah, Buddy—knows me as her owner. You are still a stranger to her."

Morris struggled to be patient. He and Buddy spent the next few days getting to know one another. She slept on the rug in his room. She stayed at his feet under the table when he ate. She followed him into the bathroom. They lived together. But still they did not go out with the harness.

Jack taught Morris, "Keep Buddy at your side. From now on you must feed her by yourself twice a day and take her outside to relieve herself four times a day. Every time she does what she is supposed to do, you must say, 'Buddy, atta good girl.'"

Morris did what he was told. Buddy responded. But he had imagined his dog would be wild with love for him. The only time she eagerly wagged her tail was when *Jack* entered the room. For Morris, she just stood at his side and waited for commands.

6

So Much to Remember!

Finally the day for exploring arrived. Morris fastened the harness on Buddy. He did not pinch her. He now knew where her paws were; he did not step on them. Off the two of them went across the lawn.

At afternoon tea, as Buddy sat at his feet, Morris told Mrs. Eustis, "The harness came alive in my hands. After years of fumbling with a cane at a slow pace, I felt like I was floating across the yard with Buddy. I could feel every movement of her shoulders as she walked."

Morris smiled. Then he laughed. He was free!

But this was hard work, too. Jack taught him to lengthen his stride. He yelled at Morris to remind him of everything. And there was so much to remember!

Each day Jack followed a few yards behind Buddy

and Morris, shouting instructions. "Hold your harness in the left hand! Keep your right arm close to your body, or you'll bump into things!" Jack would watch for a while, then start in again. "Morris, keep your shoulders back! Look forward! Stand tall! And always follow Buddy."

They spent many days exploring the Eustis estate. Then one day they left Fortunate Fields and headed toward town. Buddy and Morris zipped along at a smooth, quick pace. Jack followed. Buddy hesitated at one point. But Morris did not. His mind was elsewhere.

BANG!

Morris slammed into a gatepost.

Jack guffawed and continued to bellow his endless commands. "I cannot keep reminding you, Morris. Pay attention! Remember to follow your dog. She is your leader now."

The three walked to the cable car station and rode into Vevey, where they walked up and down the hilly streets. Jack continued to remind Morris to keep his body in the correct posture, to hold the harness right, and to keep his mind focused on his dog's signals. Any small hesitation from Buddy could be a

critical message for Morris. Any slack in the harness meant a change in direction or that there was an obstacle in the path ahead.

Buddy was trained to pull back and stand still at curbs so that Morris could find the edge with his foot. When they came to steps, Buddy had learned to sit down. She was also trained to anticipate trouble. If Morris was headed toward a low-hanging branch, she would take him around it, even though Morris's command had been "Forward." This was called "intelligent disobedience."

Buddy moved fast as she guided Morris. She had learned to judge how much space was required for him. She had also learned to ignore other dogs and interesting diversions while she worked. Buddy was trained to think for herself and to take care of her owner.

7

Together

By the end of that first afternoon together in Vevey, Morris's feet hurt. His left arm was sore. His back muscles were begging for a rest. In the little town, Morris had bumped his knees and skinned his shins. Keeping up with the dog's fast pace had been a challenge. Sometimes he had not listened to the traffic. He had not given Buddy his complete attention and trust.

When he and Buddy returned to Fortunate Fields, Morris did not feel like visiting with the others. He did not want to eat dinner. He went to his room in despair. Morris was afraid he would never figure out how to work with a guide dog, let alone teach others.

Jack visited Morris in his room. He said, "Stop feeling sorry for yourself! You have a dog. Think of the

blind people back in America who are always waiting for someone to help them, the ones who must rely on others' charity, the ones whose only opportunity for work is to make brooms or weave baskets. These people are waiting for independence. They are waiting for you!" Jack paced up and down the room and continued, "No one said this would be easy, Morris, but you have an opportunity—to make life different for yourself and for others."

Jack stopped talking. Then Morris heard the door open and close. He was alone.

Morris sat on his bed, full of doubt. He wanted to help others, but first he had to succeed himself. He was not sure he could.

As if she could read his mind, Buddy slipped onto his bed. She sniffed his ear. She licked his cheek.

Then Morris understood. He and Buddy were a team. *She* knew what to do; he was still learning. She would show him the way. He just had to trust her. They would succeed, together!

8
Runaways

Morris and Buddy trained together for a few more weeks. One day Morris realized he needed a haircut. He asked Jack to take him into town. Mrs. Eustis overheard and said, "You can get a haircut by yourself. With Buddy by your side, you can go anywhere!"

At home Morris's father often left him with the barber in the morning. Morris waited there for hours until his father could pick him up at lunchtime. Now, with his dog, he did not have to wait. Morris could perform this ordinary task without help. He harnessed Buddy, and the two of them walked to the cable car together.

When Buddy paused at the curb, Morris felt with his foot for the edge. When she pulled him to the side to avoid a hole, he followed her lead. While he sat in the barber's chair, she lay at his feet and waited for his commands. When the haircut was done, Morris and Buddy returned to Fortunate Fields with ease.

As the days passed, Buddy slept on Morris's bed every night. At meals she rested her head on his foot. He brushed her and fed her himself. Morris now knew every inch of her beautiful body.

She woke him each morning with a warm lick on his face and led him wherever he wanted to go. They trusted each other.

One final experience made Morris and Jack sure of their success. Near the end of Morris's stay in Switzerland, he and Buddy headed into town ahead of Jack. From behind him, Morris heard the clattering of hooves and a thunderous noise. His dog hesitated and then turned sharply to the right. She rushed Morris up a steep muddy hill.

When the clattering passed, Jack raced to them. Breathing hard, he said, "You could have been killed! If I had any lingering doubts about your dog, they have disappeared now. That dog just saved you from runaway horses that were dragging a wagon. You would have been crushed if Buddy had not been so aware."

9

Crossing Death Street

Morris and Buddy were ready to return to the United States. Ahead of them lay the biggest adventure of their lives—starting a guide dog school for the blind.

Before they left Fortunate Fields, Dorothy Eustis met with Morris. She said there were two things he must do before a school could be started in America.

First, he must demonstrate that a guide dog was as safe as a human guide, especially in traffic. He must do this by crossing busy streets in several American cities. Publicity would be important for spreading the word.

Second, he must get dogs accepted in public places. "No dogs allowed" signs were everywhere, but a guide dog is useless if it is not allowed to guide wherever people go. Morris had to begin the battle to get guide dogs accepted everywhere.

Morris and Buddy boarded a steamer headed for New York City. This time Morris was free to go to the dining room on his own. He visited with people in the evenings. For exercise he and Buddy walked on the deck in the afternoons. And when he was ready to go to bed, they made their way to their room without help.

When the boat landed in New York on June 11, 1928, there was a crowd of reporters sent to cover ship arrivals. Morris began to brag to them about his dog.

"You're sure you and your dog can go anywhere we can?" asked one reporter.

"I'm sure," insisted Morris.

"Then cross West Street."

"It's a deal!" said Morris. He did not know this nearby street, but it was so wide and the traffic so heavy that it was known as Death Street. Some of the reporters tried to dissuade him. But Morris had confidence in Buddy.

The reporters followed Morris into the bustling New York crowd.

"Buddy, forward," he said.

Morris could feel Buddy's head move from side to

side as she watched the traffic. There were no stoplights on this busy street, so she carefully led him forward. She halted. She stepped. She stopped. Morris almost lost his balance. The stiff leather harness gave him every message of movement or hesitation.

Morris could feel the whoosh of air as trucks and automobiles rushed past. The smell from nearby restaurants and the blaring, screeching, honking city noises overwhelmed his senses as he contemplated what was racing by. Yet as he later wrote in his autobiography, *First Lady of the Seeing Eye,* "Buddy was as calm as if she were at home in her quiet little Swiss village."

Finally he felt the far curb and knew that they had made it. He knelt down and hugged his dog. "Buddy, atta good girl," said Morris.

The reporter who had made the bet ran to Morris. "By gosh, you crossed that street! It took a long time, but you did it. I had to hail a taxi to get here!"

Morris had gotten the first publicity for his American guide dog school.

Afterword

$\mathcal{M}$orris returned to his home in Nashville, where he set up the guide dog school. There were two students in the first class in 1929. By the end of that year, seventeen people had been trained.

Dorothy Eustis donated money and sent Jack Humphrey and a new young trainer named Adelaide Clifford. The school was named The Seeing Eye and was moved in 1931 to New Jersey. It moved to its present location outside of Morristown, New Jersey, in 1965. The Seeing Eye has now placed more than fourteen thousand dogs and continues to provide dogs and lifetime training to qualified people.

Buddy lived for ten more years. Although Morris received more dogs, all of whom he also named Buddy, his first remained special in his heart. Morris married and spent many years working with The Seeing Eye. He traveled extensively, giving speeches and fighting for acceptance of blind people and their guide dogs. Starting in Nashville, he and Buddy introduced people to the idea of guide dogs in restaurants, on trolleys, and in other public places. By 1935 all the major railroads permitted guide dogs to ride with their owners, and in 1938 United Airlines agreed to allow guide dogs in the cabin. Morris Frank died on November 22, 1980.

In 1990 the Americans with Disabilities Act was passed. This law stated that people with special needs could not be discriminated against because of their condition. Now not only are guide dogs and other helper dogs permitted on trains and airplanes and in stores, hotels, and restaurants, but various accommodations are also made in public places for hearing-impaired people, people in wheelchairs, and others with special needs.

Morris Frank started this process in 1927 when he wrote his letter to Dorothy Eustis, asking her to help him so that he could help others.

Morris Frank striding confidently with Buddy, about 1950.

Jack Humphrey, Dorothy Eustis,
Morris Frank, and Buddy at
Mrs. Eustis's estate, Fortunate Fields
in Vevey, Switzerland, 1928.

Morris and Buddy
walking through
Vevey, 1928.

The first training class of The Seeing Eye in Nashville, February 1929. From the left: Jack Humphrey (head instructor); Dr. Raymond Harris (student) and his dog, Tartar; Adelaide Clifford (instructor); Dr. Howard Buchanan (student) and his dog, Gala; and Willi Ebeling (instructor).

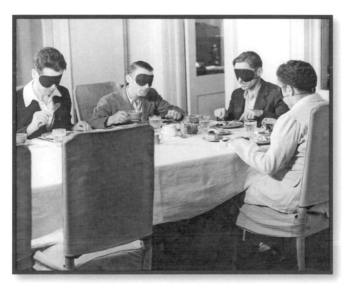

Instructors in training at dinner, 1934. The Seeing Eye expects instructor trainees to wear blindfolds for a week to better understand the difficulties their students will encounter in daily life. At meals, different foods are placed on the plate in a clockwise position to make it easy to find where everything is located.

Instructor William Debetaz trains a dog to avoid an obstacle that the blind person might encounter (1934). The dogs must learn to think as if they were the height of their owners.

Morris and Buddy board a United Airlines plane soon after the airline agreed to permit guide dogs to fly. They traveled all over the country so Morris could give speeches and meet graduates from The Seeing Eye. Buddy died soon after this photo was taken in 1939.

A dog in training places its body between instructor Drew Gibbon and open railroad tracks. The dogs learn "intelligent disobedience," which means this dog would have disobeyed a command to go forward into a situation dangerous for his owner.

A young puppy raiser with her dog. Puppies are born at the The Seeing Eye headquarters in Morristown, New Jersey. Then they are raised by foster families until they are fourteen to eighteen months old. In the foster homes, the dogs bond with humans. They learn basic obedience and appropriate behavior in public. Foster care is done in conjunction with the 4H Youth Development Program.

Bibliography

Alexander, Sally Hobart. *Mom's Best Friend*. New York: Macmillan, 1992.

Arnold, Caroline. *A Guide Dog Puppy Grows Up*. New York: Harcourt Brace Jovanovich, 1991.

Bergman, Thomas. *Seeing in Special Ways: Children Living with Blindness*. Milwaukee: Gareth Stevens, 1989.

Carter, Alden R. *Seeing Things My Way*. Morton Grove, Ill.: Albert Whitman, 1998.

Edwards, Nicola. *My Friend Is Blind*. North Mankato, Minn.: Smart Apple Media, 2005.

Eustis, Dorothy Harrison. *Dogs As Guides for the Blind*. Lausanne, Switzerland: Imprimerie Delacoste-Borgeaud, October 1929. The text of this booklet can be found on the web site www.seeingeye.org under "Resource Center" and then under "Reading Room" (2006, August 15).

Eustis, Dorothy Harrison. "The Seeing Eye." *Saturday Evening Post*, November 5, 1927, pp. 43-45. See www.seeingeye.org under "Resource Center" and then under "Press Kit" (2006, August 15).

Frank, Morris. Letter to Dorothy Eustis, November 9, 1927. See www.seeingeye.org under "Resource Center" and then under "Press Kit" (2006, August 15).

Frank, Morris, and Blake Clark. *First Lady of the Seeing Eye*. New York: Henry Holt, 1957.

Hartwell, Dickson. *Dogs Against Darkness: The Story of the Seeing Eye*. New York: Dodd, Mead, 1960.

Humphrey, Elliott, and Lucien Warner. *Working Dogs*. Baltimore: Johns Hopkins University Press, 1934. Reprint, Wenatchee, Wash.: Dogwise Publishing, 2005.

McDaniel, Melissa. *Guide Dogs*. New York: Bearport, 2005.

McMahon, Patricia. *Listen for the Bus: David's Story*. Honesdale, Pa.: Boyd's Mills Press, 1995.

Mooney, Bill. "With a Dog's Eyes: Capturing the Life of Morris Frank." In this one-man play, available on video from The Seeing Eye, Mooney portrays Morris Frank.

Moore, Eva. *Buddy, the First Seeing Eye Dog*. New York: Scholastic, 1996.

Patent, Dorothy Hinshaw. *The Right Dog for the Job: Ira's Path from Service Dog to Guide Dog*. New York: Walker, 2004.

Putnam, Peter Brock. *Love in the Lead: The Miracle of the Seeing Eye*. New York: University Press of America, 1997.

Putnam, Peter Brock. *Triumph of the Seeing Eye*. New York: Harper & Row, 1963.

Swanbeck, Steve. *The Seeing Eye*. Charleston, S.C.: Arcadia Publishing, 2002.

WEB SITES

American Federation for the Blind. www.afb.org (2006, August 15).

Guide Dog Origins. www.guidedog.org (2006, August 15).

The Seeing Eye. www.seeingeye.org (2006, August 15).